SHOPIFY

How To Create Your Online Empire! E-Commerce, Drop Shipping and Making Money Online

By: Greg Addison

Free Bonus: Join Our Book Club and Receive Free Gifts Instantly

Click Below For Your Bonus:
https://success321.leadpages.co/freebo dymindsoul/

TABLE OF CONTENTS

INTRODUCTION

In the past few years, the number of people opting for online business has increased tremendously. The primary reason for this is not just the convenience to work from home, but also the good amount of money one can earn sitting at home. Whether it's a small product costing a few dollars or a highly expensive product, people first do an online search as it provides them with a variety of options all available at one place. Moreover, it also saves the customer from moving out and searching for an item at a number of stores. Who would like to go outside and search for a single item when one can get the stuff at home? Apart from this, the person also gets all the specifications of the product as well as the payment security. By this, nothing remains in confusion and people simply love to do online shopping.

Now, how about selling your own items online! Yes, it sounds a wonderful opportunity as you would be able to entertain the ever increasing number of online customers and with that, your income will also increase.

There are some wonderful options like Shopify which gives a platform to sell your products online and earn handsome amount.

So, are you also eager to set up your online business, but feeling confused due to less knowledge about it? Then, no need to worry at all! Choose Shopify to see your products and they will provide you everything. Right from hosting, domain and designing to CMC and payment gateways, Shopify offers everything one requires to start a successful store online.

Yes, it's a professional e-commerce platform, in fact, one of the best sites at present which can be used to make great amount even if you are a newbie in this field.

And, can you imagine the number of people using Shopify to sell their stuff? It's more than 70,000 which also include some renowned brands. Some of the world famous companies using Shopify are Evernote, Pixar, Amnesty International, General Electric and Wikipedia.

Not just a few, but tons of people realized their dream of becoming millionaires with Shopify. It follows the simple formula which says more work and more sales means more money.

With a plethora of options available with Shopify, you are also provided with a number of shipping options. The professionally designed themes offered by the site also add to the interest in your site store.

And now the most important question which must be hovering in your mind till now. How much does it cost to sell on Shopify? Hope I guessed it right! So, leave all your worries here as Shopify is cheap beyond your expectations. We will certainly discuss the answer to this question in detail in the following chapters. Here, in short, we can say that Shopify charges only 1.5% of your sales, and that's undoubtedly a great price. Not only this, but you also get a 14-day trial package, and if you don't like the site, you can quit without any charges.

Selling your products online is only becoming easier as the years go by. Shopify is easily the best of the various ecommerce websites out there, but it's not the only one. However, if you're looking for a website that's affordable, easy to use, and creative, then Shopify is the one for you.

CHAPTER ONE

THE BEGINNER'S GUIDE TO SHOPIFY

Have you decided to start your online business with the online sale of products? Then, Shopify is the one stop solution. Interested in selling small or big products or any services, Shopify is certainly the best e-commerce plan which one must consider. Be it any kind of business and of any size, it easily caters to every business' requirements. In case you are planning to open your online store for the first time, Shopify is definitely the easiest e-commerce builder to help you making the process painless and straightforward. Here we will discuss using Shopify's platform right from your decision to use it to your launching your own online store with its usage.

You would be glad to know that if you've already decided to do your business using Shopify, then you may also get an exciting welcome with the Shopify discount code generally available for new users.

What is E-Commerce?

In case you haven't heard the term e-commerce before, here's a quick rundown of what it means. Essentially, it is the term coined for making any sort of transaction online. This is usually done on a website that has been optimized for e-commerce transactions. For example, a site like Amazon is an e-commerce site. You go on and you browse through their collection. Then, you find something you want, add it to your cart, fill in all the necessary information, and you'll receive your product within a few days.

E-commerce is great way to find something online that you might not otherwise find in a store. It's also a lot more convenient, since you can get the items delivered straight to your door. It makes it much easier and less work for you.

Every online transaction that you make is a part of e-commerce. However, there is a little more to it than simply online transactions. With the invention of smartphones, mobile commerce has taken off. While it's the same as e-commerce on the surface, it has become its own independent part of the online market. Mobile commerce is growing every day and might one day be more popular than buying something on a computer.

Where did Shopify Originate?

You might be wondering where exactly Shopify came from. It originated from Canada with Tobias Lütke, Daniel Weinand, and Scott Lake. They originally wanted to make a website in order to sell snowboarding equipment. This became the basis for their newer website, Shopify. You can still access the other website, called Snowdevil, but it's only a demo site. You can't buy anything and you won't be charged if you do try to buy something.

Shopify has grown exponentially since its launch back in 2006. The great thing about this is that you don't have to own a business to use this resource. You can sell things from home if you so desire. This makes Shopify a great way to sell things that you make. This can be the start of a business, but it doesn't have to be.

Shopify also has an app that you can download to keep up to date with your store and see what you've sold. This is a great tool to use when you aren't home and don't have access to a computer. This app will keep you informed of everything, in real time, going on with your store. It might be one of the most useful tools that Shopify has to offer.

Understanding What You Can Sell on Shopify

In short, we can say that any such product which is considered legal to be sold online can be sole using the medium of Shopify. And this may include any physical product, digital product or any drop ship product and service. To understand this in a better manner, you can check the sitemap of Shopify and check the "Ecommerce by Industry" section. There, you can see the most popular verticals using the platform of Shopify clearly listed. Almost everything can be seen in that list including artworks, e-books, guitars, shoes, and homewares. In fact, it's hard to point out something which can't be sold there.

In case you have your own offline physical retail store, you can also merge and manage all your sales and inventory system at one location which is fantastically done with POS which refers to Shopify's Point of Sale System. This is perfect for any small business owners who want a secure way to handle their sales.

The fact that you can have a physical store outside of the internet and still use Shopify is very impressive. Suddenly, small, family owned businesses have a great way to keep track of their employees and the sales they are making. The POS system is a great way to not only expand Shopify's network, but also for basically anyone with things to sell able to access Shopify.

Pricing Details of Shopify

What's the best part about Shopify which attracts everyone to do business with it? It's certainly Shopify's flexible pricing plan which meets everyone's requirements without digging a hole in their pocket. It's easy and low-cost plans helps businesses of all sizes to flourish on its platform.

Basically, there are 4 primary pricing tiers which are priced as per the functionality and e-commerce features and tools available for you to grow your online business. The higher priced tier also offers an additional enterprise-grade solution which is mainly available for larger businesses.

The cheapest of all the plans is the Lite plan which charges $9 per month. Next is the basic plan which is of $29 per month. Then, you have the professional plan which you can have for $79 per month. Next is the unlimited plan available for $179 per month and the last and the highest is the Shopify Plus which charges $995 per month.

The best part is none of the Shopify plans charge any setup fee, but all the plans offer unlimited product uploads and file storage facility. Not only this, but you also get 24/7 online and phone support. Apart from this, no bandwidth fees and no transaction fees are charged during the usage of Shopify payments. In each plan, you get options to add website templates and apps from the Shopify store with a plethora of selections available in both free and paid options.

All the available Shopify plans are available on a monthly basis unless you choose the option of a biennial or an annual plan. So, you can easily downgrade, upgrade or cancel Shopify any time.

Not only this, Shopify provides high discounts on the payment of upfront fees. There is 10% discount offered on annual plans and 20% off on biennial plans. Apart from this, you also get a Shopify discount code on signing up.

Comparison of Shopify with Other Platforms

So, how is the Shopify experience better than other e-commerce platforms? In simple terms, Shopify is far more creative as compared to other platforms. The most beneficial thing which Shopify offers and other platforms do not is Shopify POS which helps in the synchronization of physical store locations with their online and offline sales.

Some other sites are Bigcommerce and Volusion are the biggest competitors for Shopify. Out of the three, Shopify has the best ratings and most features that are perfect for your e-commerce website. Plus, there's an added bonus of this having the lowest price basic model. These three sites have many things that are always put head to head.

The ease of set-up is very easy in Shopify, especially compared to the others. There are tons of great features, including the fact that it asks you if you're moving from another platform. This allows you to import everything that you had on the other site onto your Shopify site, making it a lot easier to quickly set up your shop.

When comparing this to Volusion, you'll see that Volusion is fairly simple to setup, but it's both not as visually pleasing and you need to have some coding experience. Having coding experience definitely isn't the top priority for many people who are trying to start a business.

As for Bigcommerce, there are a lot of great features to help you setup your website in minutes. However, there isn't a drag and drop feature, so that does take some time away from how quickly you can set it up. Also, the dashboard itself looks very similar to that of Shopify.

There are a ton of add-ons and apps available for Shopify. The same can't be said for some of the other e-commerce sites available. These add-ons and apps are easy to find in Shopify, as you can just search through the hundreds of apps that are there.

Bigcommerce is another one that has a multitude of apps and add-ons. Like with Shopify, it also has a way to search through these apps to find exactly what you're looking for, whether it's an app to build a loyalty program or something else.

This makes Shopify and Bigcommerce the best options for apps and add-ons.

Volusion, however, definitely isn't worth it if this is something you look at closely. There is only one app offered, so if that isn't something you are super excited about or something you need, look elsewhere. You'll only be wasting money if you want apps and choose Volusion.

Speaking of money, the price you need to pay in order to get your e-commerce site is pretty important. Shopify, out of these three, is easily the best option. The cheapest option for Shopify is 9 dollars. For Volusion, it's 15 dollars, which is six dollars more. Finally, for Bigcommerce, the cheapest option is almost 30 dollars.

For the middle pricing, once again, Shopify is the winner. It's only 29 dollars for their middle, while its 35 for Volusion and almost 80 for Bigcommerce. As for the most expensive, however, Volusion is the winner. For Shopify, the price is 299. Bigcommerce is a whopping 900 or more. Volusion is a respectable 135. That being said, Volusion is also the one with the least number of extra features. This is a great one to do if you are a small business that doesn't really plan on expanding or doing anything crazy. However, if you want to do more, it would be better to choose another option.

Shopify does have the best prices overall when you compare how many features you're getting with the price. Bigcommerce also has a lot of features, but many of them are the same as the ones in Shopify, so it doesn't entirely seem worth it.

One thing that might not be all that good about Bigcommerce is that if you exceed a certain number of sales in a year, you will be forced to upgrade your account to one that you need to pay a lot more for. Even if this is the first year your business is open, if it exceeds the allotted sales on the basic one, you'll be paying a few hundred dollars a month. This really isn't beneficial for new businesses. Just because you have one year that's very good doesn't mean every year will be just as good.

Volusion is the only one to have a cap on how many products you can have in your store and how much bandwidth you can use. For just starting out, Volusion might be a good choice, but as you get further along in your business, you'll want to be able to expand. Having unlimited spots for products is the best way to do just that.

When looking at all three, Bigcommerce and Shopify are actually pretty similar. Each has their own unique features that the other doesn't have, though one is more pricey than the other. Volusion, on the other hand, isn't good for a business that plans on rapidly expanding. It is, however, great for a small business that might just be extra income for the family who owns it.

Out of all three of these, Shopify is the most popular one that people choose to use. With the features and lower prices, it is a great choice for anyone who wants room to grow in their business.

Is Shopify Worth It?

One thing you need to know before deciding that Shopify is the store for you is that it takes care of everything you need it to. All you need to do is have the product and have the sense of how to run your business.

Also, there are a few different ways to sell your products. The first is, of course, selling things online. This can be used on the website that you create with Shopify and will allow you to sell your items on your website. All you'll need to do is customize the website to what you desire and add your products. The checkout page is seamless and very easy for customers to use.

Next, there's Shopify POS, which is Point of Sale. This will allow you to sell an item no matter where you are. You can get a handy card reader device that allows you to swipe, use it for cards with chips, or touch pay. There's also a mobile app that goes with this, which will allow you to know everything about your shop with the click of a button. Also, all of your data is automatically synched between your app and the website. If you make a sale, it will show up within seconds.

If you have a store location, you can still take advantage of everything Shopify has to offer. You can receive a number of different pieces of hardware to help you with your business journey, including a cash drawer, card reader, receipt printer, iPad stand, and a barcode scanner. This is perfect for people who have multiple staff members. You can actually find out what products your staff members are selling and see how much each one is selling. Each member will have a unique pin linked to their account, which you can access.

Finally, there's the buy button. If you have products that you sell on Tumblr, WordPress, Squarespace, or many other websites, you can embed a code onto your website that will allow people to buy off of that site. If you use something like Facebook or Pinterest for your products, you can still sell them on there as well. Your customers will have the ability to stay on that website and buy whatever they want through a secure checkout system. All of this is to make your business much easier to manage.

These various options will make your days of looking for a way to sell your products online much easier. Shopify makes it easy for anyone who sells products to find the right fit for them.

In fact, there are a crazy number of benefits in Shopify that you can't find in sites like BigCommerce and Volusion, which are Shopify's biggest competitors.

1. Speed

The websites you can create on Shopify are incredibly fast. Customers will be able to easily load the page and click on anything they want without worrying about long loading times. There have been plenty of studies done on how long a customer will wait for a web page to load before going somewhere else. On average, they will wait a total of four seconds, which really isn't a lot of time.

Shopify, however, makes sure that the loading times are fast and convenient for both you and your customer. You'll never have to worry about losing a customer to slow loading times.

2. Features

What features do you think of when looking for an online way to sell your products? A way to easily add and remove products, easily customizing the look of your shop, and integrating an analytics page without too much hassle might be at the top of your list. Shopify makes all of these things simple to do.

Not to mention, marketing your shop and products has never been easier. Shopify has integrated SEO features, ways to make discount codes for your products, gift cards, and targeting email marketing, among other things. The amount of features that Shopify has to offer is impressive and might help make up your mind.

3. Customer Support

Starting out with something like Shopify can be incredibly confusing. There are tons of options and different things to choose from. How are you supposed to know exactly what to do right from the beginning?

The customer support provided on Shopify is incredibly helpful. This will not only help you understand everything you need in the beginning, but is a great resource to go back to when you have a question in the future. There are FAQ's, email and chat support, and some phone support as well. These are all great ways to figure out what you need to know in an easy and un-confusing way.

4. Security

If you're making your website from scratch, you'll need to have something that can protect it from hackers, especially if you have a website where you're selling items. In Shopify, the security of your site is already taken care of.

Shopify has all of the tools necessary to completely protect your website from anything malicious. There are plenty of security updates to make sure that there are no holes in security, something startup businesses have to constantly worry about. With Shopify, that's taken out of the equation. You can focus on setting up your website rather than worrying about any potential breaches.

5. Design

There are tons of design options available in Shopify. If you have a specific vision for what you want your website to look like, you're more than likely able to find it in Shopify. It's crazy just how easy it is to get the look you want.

Even if you aren't entirely sure what you want it to look like, every design option is visually appealing. There are tons of basic themes available at the start, which are a great way to begin with. If you aren't satisfied with the basic themes or want to upgrade, there are also tons of paid themes that you can look through.

Many of these themes give you the ability to look at previews for desktop, mobile, and tablet, so you'll be able to see exactly what it will look like on whatever device someone will look at.

6. Website Hosting

You might not realize it, but the fact that you only pay a little money every month for having a website hosted is pretty awesome. You could rent your own server and be paying a lot of money, but with Shopify, the server is taken care of for you. Everything becomes a lot easier and stress-free when you don't have to worry about server costs.

This also means that you don't have to make sure the server is running smoothly. Shopify takes the reins and makes sure your server is working for you. You also don't have to download any software onto your computer to make all of this work, which also makes it even easier.

Shopify is full of various features and apps that will make your life of owning an online business much easier. You won't have to worry about anything like hosting or security. You can focus entirely on adding products and making your shop page look sleek and visually appealing. Shopify is easily the best e-commerce way to make your business dreams come true.

CHAPTER TWO

HOW TO DRIVE TRAFFIC TO YOUR SHOPIFY SITE

Launching your own store is a onetime process. It is an opportunity for you to draw as much traffic and attention as you can. There are certain things or steps which you can take to get more traffic drawn towards your store during its grand inauguration. This will further help you in becoming a seasoned marketer with huge sales.

In this article, you will get to know more about how to get traffic for your new store with the help of influencers and drawing attention. Here we provide six templates and some tactics which will help you for your store's campaign. You can just copy and paste these templates. By the end of this chapter, you will also gain some valuable information and things which will help you in maintaining the momentum of a well-established business.

Let's start with the six different templates used to gain traffic.

1. Provide Free samples to Instagram Users

One of the most loved social media applications Instagram is certainly considered to be a very efficient marketing channel for ecommerce merchants. As per the findings of a recent study, Instagram is a fast growing social platform which enhances the customer to reach of a brand by 25% than any other social platform does. Our own analysis proves that it generates a much higher average order value when compared to Facebook, Google Plus, Pinterest, and Twitter. It helps in driving a lot of traffic to your store when you know how to draw the influencer's attention. For example, let's assume that you are willing to start an online skin care product company.

- From where should you start promoting your products and gain attention for your store?

You can start by searching for popular accounts on Instagram that will allow you to feature your products to their followers.

- How will you find such accounts?

You can search with the help of WEBSTA. It is a website which records all the popular hashtags and account users on Instagram. You can easily locate these popular users and hashtags by just typing 'skincare' in the search bar. This will redirect you to those users who have the term 'skincare' mentioned in their bio or username. With the help of this, you can get the link to that user's contact page, email, and phone number.

You can also use the mobile app of Instagram for targeting the influencers. You can go through the popular pages on Instagram which contains the latest trending pictures. Click on any such trending picture to get the username or link of the user's account. Look for contact details like email in the bio of the user.

These users often provide their email address for advertisement, product placement, and partnership opportunities. After this, you have people's reach which has to be strategic. Not all users have a huge amount of followers. Targeting the perfect user for getting the job done is the most important part.

- What is a reach out campaign?

Suppose that you have targeted a user who has mentioned his/her business address. The next thing for you is to send a sample along with a note which describes your product. If there is no business address provided then send a note, asking whether the user is interested in featuring certain skincare products or not.

2. Get connected to press and bloggers

You can easily reach out to people like bloggers and vloggers who have a certain amount of followers on various websites and social media platforms. The process of contacting them is quite similar as contacting Instagram influencers.

Google can be the source for searching a blogger.

Pick some relevant keywords like 'skincare tips,' 'skincare methods' and 'skin care' to search on YouTube. Go through the videos posted on YouTube and check whether they post regularly or not. You may have to watch multiple videos before contacting anyone who will actually feature your product. You will find many people who take this as their mode of earning.

Another good option for gathering huge traffic is the press. You might not get an opportunity to have your product published by a big newspaper, but you will get a scope to introduce your product to the press or local news site. If you can come up with some unique ideas and brilliant descriptions about your product, then there stands a chance for you to get your product featured. Construct a short, but effective pitch for your product as reporters have to go through a lot of pitches. Short and unique pitches are always welcomed to take up as a success story.

Just like any Instagram personality can give your product optimum exposure, a popular blogger, vlogger or the press can do the same if they agree to feature your product. It will help in drawing traffic, maximizing sales and gaining attention. Just as you can send a sample and a note to an Instagram user, similarly you can get in touch with a blogger or press.

What should you write to a blogger, vlogger or press?
This template will help you to get things started and sorted. To be published as a success story you can pitch for it. Prepare a note which you will like to send to the appropriate person. There are many people with huge audiences, and they gain a lot of attention while you are waiting for your shot at getting the success story covered. There is no such rule that you have to opt for the most successful and biggest people. You can opt for people with less amount of audience as they are not always crowded by people similar to you, looking to get featured. For your information, the retro video game seller, Chris Dammacco targets vloggers will small audiences on YouTube. One thing which matters the most is the loyalty of the audience which is much similar to the size of the audience.

3. Reddit your store

Reddit is basically the hangout hub for the internet users. Along with the main page of Reddit, there are multiple numbers of niches known as the subreddits. It a cumulative source of the most popular contents trending on the internet. You can search for a subreddit by just typing /r/sci-fi, /r/swimming, /r/gaming, etc. to help you and your store, you should follow some threads.

The first thing which everyone should be surfing is /r/entrepreneur subreddit. It has several interesting tips, facts, and discussions based on entrepreneurship made by its 79,000 subscribers. You will also find some threads like /r/small business which will fetch general information on business tactics. Give a brief description on your store and products. Give a catchy headline like, *"Health care starts with skin care. My store brings you the best of skin care products for all types of skin."*

Keep it short, effective, snappy but not sale-y. To know whether you are following the guidelines of Reddit, you can go through the Reddiquette guide. Check the subreddit rules which can be found in the right sidebar of subreddit. There are certain subreddits which do not allow posting promotional posts. So, what's an ad for you is a big no-no for them? Even if you are posting about your site in a subreddit which doesn't entertain such posts, you will be facing certain consequences like getting banned from the subreddit. Kindly follow the rules before posting anything.

4. Ask your friend and family to share:

Are you already in that age where all your friends are posting pictures of their children and is it annoying when all you can think about is work? Well, there are people who do get sick of baby photos, but you can surely give them relief by selling your online store! People don't launch a startup very often, so you have high chances to make your work get an added eye within your circle of people.

Have you heard of Upworthy? I am sure you have! Their articles are all over our Facebook feed. You'd be surprised to know that their initial traffic generation happened with the help of their friends and families. They had a goal to get around 1,000 Facebook likes, and by the end of their first day, it actually worked out! This was the part that gave them their initial traction and everything took off. Things started rolling in, and it became a popular name. Thus, ask your well-wishers to do you an initial aid without making them feel irritated.

When you are on Facebook, talk about your store through updates. Talk to your family, extended family, relatives, and friends. Have them reunited through mails and send them a note about your store. They will not only share your work but also refer other people when they know someone who could need you. Don't stress on selling your products, but sell your concepts and show them how unique you are. Ask them to make simple promotions through sharing and networking. These people will be able to share your work and give you success by reaching out to the mutual and also the non-mutual people on your list.

5. Engaging on Twitter proactively:

You don't really need to start selling before you have started engaging people onto your Twitter account. There are several ways to get people in your store. For example, Blackbird Baking Company from Toronto is a bakery that sells fresh bread. They had over 500 followers before their store had opened! If you have a few hundred people before you launch, you will not solely await your big day!

Now suppose you have something similar to sell. Post about your work on Twitter and see how people are reacting to it. You will be redirected to people who are interested in having a new bakery, and you are likely to get some restaurateurs and self-declared bread enthusiasts in your region!

Followerwonk is one tool that can be used for finding some relevant users who could be interested in following your page. As soon as you log onto Twitter, you will get relevant keywords, and you can browse through bios and profiles. This process helps you follow a neat tweeting strategy. The Blackbird baking company has been flourishing over the months and is selling their goods to interested stores across Toronto. They have also been adding several pictures on Instagram and Facebook which not only shows their success but also customer's interests. You should also check them out to realize how mouthwatering and shareable food could be!

It is pretty easy to active people through tweets and publicizes within your local community. You will get topics that include about the life in Toronto, their food, people and of course their bread. They have also mentioned important details like opening and closing time, new sells, etc. so you should always keep your customers updated.

Thus, the central strategy is, search for keywords in Twitter and get it related to the business. Look for several chances to introduce your work to the interested customers and higher your sales pitch. You will soon realize how valuable your tweets are to the concerned group of people!

6. **Create a blog, feature people and audience and then publicize:**

Finally, the last part of this suggestion is to reach out to prospective buyers by connecting people through big audience and blogging. Rather than sending samples of products, you are likely to get more traffic in better way – writing a blog post and send them through mail or Twitter. Don't wait for them to feature you, when you can feature them before! You are anyway looking for influencers in your concerned industry. Write about the top people that you find and turn it into an easy blog post by featuring popular Instagramers, vloggers, bloggers, etc.

Some common examples of headlines are:

- Top 10 hairstyle bloggers to follow

- Top 15 Twitter profiles to follow

- Top 20 Instagramers to discover new hairstyles

- Top 4 YouTube personalities for style tutorials

In your post, add some blurb discussing who they are as you list them one by one. Circulate the post through your Twitter account. It is important to add their handles, but don't be obvious that you require their attention. You should be thoughtful and innovative, which will draw in all their concerns!

Your store will launch once you don't have a lot of problems to reach out to people. Do whatever it takes to draw in traffic and then turn visitors into customers. Once this is done, move towards your online store and work on it.

It is important to remember than drawing traffic is a continuous process, and you must stick to it. Even if you think you have enough followers, it is actually never enough. Keep engaging people so that you can market yourself a little every moment. You will soon have a pool of followers, and that might make you feel that it is enough, but in reality, you can never have too many followers or too much traffic. This just keeps on expanding you and bettering your work. So, simply gear up for what you have ahead and embrace yourself for lots of appreciation and love!

CHAPTER THREE

CREATE YOUR ONLINE EMPIRE AND SUCCEED IN ECOMMERCE BUSINESS WITH SHOPIFY

Who wouldn't like to enjoy an online empire and do an impressive ecommerce business while sitting at home? To make your dream come true, let's first understand how to set up one's online store using Shopify.

Setting Up Your Online Store

Online store or online shopping is the latest buzz word you often get to hear. Here is an interesting offer from Shopify with a 14-day free trial that can be signed up from the main homepage. You can also click on the Free Trial button available on the menu bar. Provide your email, password and create a store name.

The URL of the page contains your store name; however, if you wish to change it later, the page allows you to change. It is always better to create a simple name which like you.myshopify.com because choosing multiple words will show the link like your-business-name.myshopify.com. In case, you don't want to be redirected to a URL from your domain like store.yourdomain.com to you.myshopify.com; then you must keep a store name/URL ready on hand. You will have to provide all your basic details such name, address, and phone number while creating your account on Shopify. After this process, you will be taken to the admin dashboard to start creating your online store. Check out the 7 steps guide to ease the process.

1. **Add your products**

Start adding products to your store by manual addition or a bulk upload from a CSV file or import from platforms like Magento and eBay. If you have digital products, then firstly you need to install an app for digital product delivery, add your products using this app. The Shopify's online manual. throws more light on the selling of digital products. If you have selling services that you are attempting to sell, then opt for an app like Product Options with which you can customize your service offerings. Shopify store allows you to have 100 variations for the products which typically have options as for size, color, and finish. This site gives you the feasibility to add a product with a set of options, and there is no limit as such if it is a physical product. For example, you have 3 options for your e-book, i.e., just the e-book, the second is e-book along with supporting material and a 3rd option which is inclusive of everything plus access to a private member forum. The Shopify Documentation clearly tells you how to set up products.

2. Customize your design

The next step is to add custom design by choosing a theme. You can choose a theme from Shopify theme store which has various designs for free as well as paid. If you do not have any plan as such and simply chose some theme, you can always edit the theme by using the template editor or theme settings editor for modifying the coding. One common place where you would want to edit is the footer because that is the space you may choose for providing social links, payment methods, and various other details.

In the next chapter, there will be some example themes that might be great to start out with. There are tons to choose from, but these ones are some of the best to look at off the bat.

3. Select Your Domain Name

The Shopify online manual encompasses all the information related to setting up of the custom domain name of your store. So, instead of being forced to choose a domain like you.myshopify.com, you can select from the options like store.yourdomain.com or yourdomain.com .

4. Set up Shipping and Tax Rates

You will be required to add taxes as well as additional shipping costs to your items and also notify Shopify about the same. Shopify would list the basic prices, but it depends on the product you sell, and you may need to customize more options.

4. Set up payments

This is the critical part of all the steps. Shopify Payments accept the credit cards if you are in USA, Canada or the UK, this facility would not require any third-party payment gateways or merchant account. Shopify incorporates other payment processing services that includes Paypal, Amazon Payments, and Google Wallet.

6. Settings

Your complete profile needs to be set up carefully, most of these details get filled while you do it step-by-step. However, it doesn't ask for the information required for adding your Google Analytics code, store description, and store title in the profile section as all this information is required to be filled in the general settings.

7. Open Your Store and Prove it to the world

Once all the details are entered, and you are ready with you online store, you can make it public. Till such time, it will be password protected, and you can also test the same to ensure if everything is functioning the way it is supposed to. Make sure that you check everything before the customer notices the loopholes.

Choosing Apps for Additional Functionality and Features

Shopify provides hundreds of free and premium apps which can be used to improvise your online store; they are categorized as:

- **Accounting** — Link your Shopify store to any of the popular accounting solutions such as Quickbooks, FreshBooks, and Xero.

- **Customer Service** — It always helps both the customer and the seller if you add contact forms, live chat, feedback, and other features for customer support.

- **Inventory** — Inventory management systems if integrated with your online store will help in the process simplification.

- **Marketing** — This category helps you include your email, search, and social media marketing into your online store.

- **Reporting** — You can check for additional analytics related to your online business with the usage of these apps. It will help you in measuring conversion rates, sales data as well as customer behavior.

- **Sales** — This category helps you in increasing the sales with the help of product reviews, customer loyalty programs, upsells, and recommendations given by others.

- **Shipping** — Create your product shipment process easier and simpler with apps that help in managing the order fulfillment process and link you with your preferred shipping service.

- **Social Media** — This is one category not to be missed on, keep yourself connected with the customers and engage them on social media platform using these apps.

- **Tools** — You will find tools that would help you in handling all the features required for running an online store successfully. The best part and the most convenient thing for the users is that it also offers setting up of bulk redirects, fighting fraud, language translators as well as RSS feeds.

Unsure of how and where to start your online store, then you may have to reconfigure your SEO settings for your product pages and in addition to that, add email marketing support so that the customers can be added to your email list. These email marketing services often guide you how to connect your Shopify store to their system.

Social Selling

This has become a totally new concept of selling and widely used these days. If you are one person who wants to sell products on your blog, then here it is. Shopify provides plugins and widgets for WordPress, Drupal and Joomla users by which you can show products in your posts, pages, and sidebar. If you are creating content based on customer's interest, this would increase traffic to your domain. Another interesting way to keep your customers in loop and engaged is to create a Facebook page and also post interesting stuff. Shopify offers various Facebook integrations that would allow you to turn your Facebook page into an e-commerce store.

What About Affiliates?

Shopify offers various apps that allow you to create your own affiliate program to keep track of referrals made by customers and supporters. You can do this if you would not mind sharing your profits with others, this will also create some publicity.

Where You Can Go to Learn More

If you are a person with zeal to learn about Ecommerce and succeed in marketing your online store, then there is no stopping. You can simply find reading material like, e-books, guides, tutorials and videos to help you learn more at Ecommerce

University. You could also check Shopify Wiki where you can go through everything you are required to know about while using Shopify and the design/development of your store. Shopify also has a support section in which you can find over 200 troubleshooting articles. Just in case, if you happen to come across some new or weird issue, you even have forums to look for support. Forums often have thousands of topics related to e-commerce.

Where You Can Get Help

This is the last resort wherein if you fail to help yourself with the troubleshooting guides, you can always seek professional help from the Shopify Experts. This area provides help with the store setup, designers, developers, marketers and photographers who can indeed make your e-commerce store into a successful business.

In this chapter, we have pretty much covered all the information required for building a successful online empire with Shopify. I am sure this would help you set up an amazing online store with the help of the tips provided here. Happy Social selling.

CHAPTER FOUR

BEST THEMES FOR STARTING OUT

Have you ever gone on a website or an online store and found everything to just not look good? Maybe things aren't where you think they should be or it just isn't visually appealing. The design for your shop could make someone continue shopping or make them turn and go somewhere else.

First, there are some general tips you should follow if you want to pick the best design for your shop.

- Stay Away from Crazy Colors

Yes, having crazy colors can be a lot of fun, no one's denying that. However, if you want someone to keep browsing through your website, you might want to stay away from them. Try to pick colors that don't clash and don't make you want to look away.

Most themes will give you good colors, but if you know coding, you can change those colors to give it a more unique feel. This is where it becomes crucial to stick with good colors. Many big online retailer sites generally have a lot of white. That can be pretty boring for a lot of people.

When you look at Amazon, it's almost entirely white, but it doesn't turn people away. People shop at Amazon not only because of the products they offer, but also because they can browse the store for long periods of time. Their eyes don't get tired and they don't feel like they need to walk away and rest.

Pick colors that are not only visually pleasing, but also go with what your store aesthetic is. You want the best that you can get for your store, so making it all come together with the colors is a great way to start.

- More Complex Navigation

You might not think about it, but depending on how many products are in your store, a simple theme might not be best. If you have twenty products, then having a simple theme will work perfectly. You'll have simple navigation and will probably be able to use just a free theme.

Since you'll need more complex navigation for the more products you have, you might have to look at paid themes instead. But, if you're just starting out, you should probably try to stick with as many free themes as possible.

- Functionality

The design is important, but it isn't necessarily the most important aspect of a theme. If the theme you have doesn't have the functions you need, then you won't be getting everything out of your store that you want.

Basically, what your store needs to do is a little more important than what it looks like. If a customer goes to your store and they can't navigate to the page they want, they'll leave. However, if you have a theme that has great navigation, then there won't be any reason for them to get confused.

Maybe you want a theme that can have things added easily. You'll want to make sure the theme does exactly that and doesn't have any problems. If it's confusing on how to add these thing to your theme, you'll probably want to find a different one. Your theme doesn't need to be difficult to use. Sometimes, the easier the theme is to use, the better it will be in the long run.

- Theme Support

Believe it or not, there is actually support for all of the themes on Shopify. Every free theme is automatically supported by Shopify, so if you ever have any problems with them, you can go to the customer support center.

Other themes will always have who the support team is. It should be on a box that has their name and how to contact them. If you know of any theme supporters who are notorious for being difficult to contact or otherwise, that is something to take into consideration. Also, if you want to have guaranteed support, maybe choosing a free theme will be best.

- Free or Paid

This is the million dollar question when choosing a theme. Is the theme you are leaning towards a paid theme? You might want to take a step back and make sure you're willing to pay for a theme, especially when you are just starting out.

Often, a free theme will be more than sufficient for a new Shopify shop owner. Buying a theme right off the bat might seem smart, but if it isn't what you wanted, then you're still stuck with it. Doing your research about every theme you look at is key. You don't want to be stuck only looking at free themes, but you also don't want to be stuck with a theme that looked good, but doesn't have that key thing you wanted.

If you want to and have the money, you can also hire someone who can create a theme customized for your store. These people are called Shopify Design Experts and they do a very good job. However, you might be forking out quite a lot of money if you aren't careful. This is best if your ideal theme is nothing like what is out there and if you have had your shop for a while.

- Who Are Your Products Targeting?

There are specific themes that will actually go with certain product types. For example, clothing and fashion might be what you are selling. If that's the case, then you can look at specific themes that are geared towards clothing and fashion.

These themes, when you go super specific, will highlight your products in the exact way that you want them to be highlighted. If you are selling electronics, many of those themes will list your products in a way that you might expect to see for electronics. Knowing what you are selling will be a huge help in making sure your theme works for your products.

Free Themes for Shopify

Shopify offers a few free themes, but not as many as you might hope. However, these themes are all great in their own ways. Some do more than you might originally think, so it's good to test all of them out and figure out which one is best for you.

Boundless

This theme is focused more on the fashion and clothing side of things. It's a very modern looking theme with a lot of great things that you can do with it. It is optimized for large product images, as these images are the first thing your customers will see.

An interesting thing about that is on the desktop version, resting your mouse on top of it will show you what the price is and the name of the product. If it's by a specific designer, their name can also go on it. After clicking on the initial image, a description of the item, various sizes, colors, the price, and numerous bigger images of the item are shown.

This is great if your item has many sides to it that should be seen. For clothing, being able to have not only a front view, but a side and back view is important. This theme will allow that to happen.

As for the different places you can go, there are plenty of navigational tabs. They can be named whatever you want, as long as they go with the products within the tab. In the demo version of this theme, there are six initial tabs. Within those, there are even more tabs to choose from. This definitely has the navigation that you would need for having tons of clothing in your store.

This theme has two different styles: black and white, and vibrant. They are set up a little differently, but both can be used for fashion and clothing. You could also use them for sports equipment, since that is generally something you'd want plenty of photos for.

This is a great option because it has SEO capabilities. It also comes with sticky navigation bar, meaning that you won't need to come back to the top of the page to go somewhere else. Also, you can have your shopping cart on the page with you as you scroll through. You'll always know how much is in your cart and how much your total is.

For a minimalist theme that's free, having sports equipment or clothing is the perfect fit. Even if you have other items, you still might be able to use this theme. As long as the large, high resolution photos are something you believe is necessary for your product, then this is the place to go.

Brooklyn

Another great theme for clothing, but it can actually accommodate a lot of different products. With a little tinkering, the different products you can feature in this store is incredible. It's a fairly simple layout, but it does a lot of great things.

It has a focus on imagery, but not as much as Boundless does. It's easy to feature certain products on the front page, but it doesn't take away from the rest of your products. They are a little lower on the page and in a cluster. Above it is links to the rest of the collection you have. These links can be done using photos of something in your products along with a label of what all the links lead to.

If you have a mailing list for your business, you can easily set up a way to have people sign up for the list. It can be done anywhere on the page and is incredibly easy for the customer. All they do is type in their email and hit enter.

This theme gives your customers the ability to share your products on any social media sites, as the social media icons are on every product page. The design of this theme is very modern and definitely feels like a place where you would sell something like clothing or maybe furniture.

There's only the default style with this theme, but it's very customizable. You'll be able to change a lot and make it look exactly like what you want, within reason. For a free theme, this has a lot of potential.

Minimal

This is another great free theme. If you want a clean, SEO optimized theme that doesn't take away from your products, this is the theme for you. In fact, this theme is one of the favorites of the free themes offered on Shopify.

This theme has three different styles: vintage, music, and fashion. Typically, you would see vintage things being sold with the vintage style, but that isn't the case with this theme. Many people will sell electronics, magazines, or other things with that style. As for the other two, you will still see people using those styles to sell things that aren't necessarily music or fashion.

This theme is not only versatile, but is also extremely easy to use. Some themes you'll find for Shopify are not the easiest for people who don't understand coding. This theme, however, is very easy to understand. You'll be able to start up your shop within minutes. For many, the initial look is perfect, but if you want to change some things around, you can do that as well.

The customization capabilities with this theme are endless. Many things can be changed, including the colors and the layout of certain items. Also, the products in this theme are really brought to light in many ways. There are photos of the products and also a description, which is a focal point of this theme.

The focus on the text about the product is crucial in this theme, which will definitely be helpful for many people. Sometimes, reading about what a product is will help them decide if they really like it. If you aren't very big into photography, then having a good description is helpful.

If you want, you can create a slideshow of some of your products on the main page. Maybe you want to put your most frequently bought items in the slideshow, as a way to showcase them even if they aren't featured. Or, maybe you can put new items or items that are on sale on that slideshow. The possibilities are endless.

For versatility, this theme definitely is one of the best. There are so many different kinds of products you can easily make fit in this theme, so it's definitely worth trying out. If your products don't quite fit, you can still choose to change up the theme a bit and see if you can make them fit. If there's a theme that is perfect for nearly everyone, this is it.

Venture

Sports equipment is a big one with this theme. You can do tons of different kinds of sports equipment, from snowboarding to golf, anything is possible. As an added bonus, this theme is perfectly meant for stores with a huge inventory. It's built to hold tons of products and the navigation won't be too hard.

The main page is extremely nice and visually pleasing. Photos dominate this theme, but they don't take away from the overall theme. The main page can also have a slideshow, showcasing certain aspects of your store. There is also a place to have a promotional banner. If you're having a sale or are trying to promote a certain product, it's a great idea to use that banner so everyone will see it. It will be the first thing they see when they click on your shop.

This theme features multi-level drop down navigation menus. If you want and easy way to go between all of your pages, this certainly makes it easier. You can have multiple pages under a certain tab that can be separated. That's what makes this theme better for larger inventories.

This theme comes with three different styles, all of which are similar. These styles are snowboards, outdoors, and boxing. They are all set up basically the same, but the color scheme of each is different. If one of them works for your store, then it's definitely a good choice.

Product filtering is also included in this theme. If you need to find something under a certain price, you'll be able to. If you need a certain type of product, you can search for that. It's great when you have a lot of products.

Venture is lacking in some areas of customization, but it has a lot to offer and you should definitely check it out. If it isn't for you, there are still tons of other ones to look at.

Debut

This would be a great theme to check out if you only have a few products. These products are usually a great way to set up your brand, which is the focus of this theme. If you came up with something like a small line of products that all go with your brand, you can showcase them with this theme.

In a way, it could be how you get your new brand out there into the world. It's not always easy when you're first starting out to find a group of people that will like your products right off the bat. So, if you use this theme, you can organize your products in a way that looks nice and will work wonderfully.

There is a header bar for the navigation bar, which makes it easy to find everything you'll need. You can also have a slideshow and a video. This is a great way to show how your products work or why they would be useful. In the demo version of this theme, there is a little video near the bottom of the page, which shows you what you might use their products for. It is a great thing for your customers to see and might just make them want to buy your product.

Is one of your products the main product you want to sell? You can feature that single product on the main page of the site. While you might not be able to feature more than one product, this theme is all about the brand. If one product really shows what your business is all about, then feature that product.

There's also the ability for your customers to hover over one of your product images and get a zoomed in view. For products with plenty of detail, this can be incredibly important to your business. That one little detail that they see might be the one that causing someone to buy your product.

Debut, like the name suggests, really works for debut companies. It's a great way to give your customers a taste of your products and see what they say about them. Then, from there, you can change the theme and add more of your products, if you have more. Definitely check it out if that's what you're going for.

Jumpstart

In many ways, this one is similar to Debut, except that this is more focused on a new product that needs some funds to be completed. Crowdfunding is becoming more popular as the years go by, so it only makes sense to have a theme that also supports that.

If you have a crowdfunding campaign going on, you can feature that on your main page. It will let your customers see how close you are to reaching your goal. Of course, this theme is also a perfect way to talk about what your product is and why it needs to be funded.

Genius ideas are always being created. Jumpstart might be the theme to use to get your product to even more audiences than ever before. If your Kickstarter page isn't getting the traffic you were hoping for, maybe using Shopify will help increase the traffic.

The demo of this theme gives you a wonderful idea of how you can use this for your crowdfunding needs. It also features a way to show what your product does in a video. Many people need to see rather than read about a product to know it's legit. Having that video can help bring more money to your crowdfunding site and expand how many people know about your product.

There are a bunch of custom modules you can choose from. If you have a blog connected to this product, you can attach that to your site. Whenever you have an update on the product and write a blog post, it will also show up on your website. This will ensure that everyone is updated in a timely fashion. You won't have to individually update every site that is attached, making your life a lot easier.

Another great thing about this theme is that it's versatile. You can have any kind of product featured with this theme and it will work. You can also have a frequently asked questions page in your website. Anything that isn't completely answered in your about page can be answered there, which will help your customers know exactly what your product is. They won't have nearly as many questions as they might have had.

Jumpstart might be the theme you need to push your product into the limelight. It's fully SEO optimized, so you'll know that people will be seeing your page if they are looking for a similar product. Just think of everything you can do with this theme and then go try it for yourself.

Supply

If electronics are your product, Supply might be the theme for you. If you have a huge inventory of electronic items, Supply is even more so the theme for you. It has a huge capacity to fill with tons of products, whether it's camera supplies or something else.

There are two presets that come with supply, which are dark and blue. They change the look of the theme just enough to give you a different feel. It's incredible how a difference in color can change the feel of the page.

Navigation is a big key when there are a lot of products in question. The more products, the harder navigation can be. Supply gives a great way to navigate between pages and to find different products in your page. You can also find products that are similar to the one you're viewing and what the top selling products are on the site. It's a great way for your customers to be exposed to everything your business has to offer.

Even though electronic devices are the most prominent, other items can also be easily implemented into these themes. Furniture might be a great one for this theme, since you can easily have over fifty products on this site.

This theme is incredibly responsive, meaning you won't lose any customers because of a slow loading page. You'll never have to worry about a page loading too slow to keep someone on your site. That is actually a lot more important than some people believe. It can be two seconds and someone will think it's too long. All of the Shopify themes are definitely responsive, which was their goal when they made them.

Supply is another aptly named theme. It's made for a huge inventory store and is definitely a theme that will keep the supply up. There are a lot of great things about this theme, but the greatest is easily the navigation. It's incredibly smooth and easy to use. Supply is a great theme for many reasons and you should definitely check it out.

Classic

Here's another theme made for big inventories. Unlike the others on this list, this has a sidebar that really makes navigation easy. This theme is mostly seen with stores that sell appliances like watches and electronics, though shoes are also a popular one.

The sidebar allows customers to narrow their search to a very specific field, like by color and size, in the case of shoes. Customers will not only find this useful, but make it much easier to find exactly what they want. This also will allow them to search by price, something that will be very beneficial to every customer.

This theme holds a lot of the values that Shopify strives for. Their biggest thing is making sure customers can browse the stores quickly and easily, without having a ton of problems. Classic is the theme that upholds that.

Classic is a great theme to check out, especially if you want your customers to have an easy time navigating your site. It will be more than worth your while.

Beauty

In case you couldn't already guess, this is a theme that's made for beauty products. Now, the name doesn't make the theme work really well, but this one definitely does. The mobile version is especially really good. It's one of the better optimized mobile versions out there and is something many people will want to look back on.

If you tend to have your business on a lot of different social media sites, you'll be able to link many of them here. You'll also be able to have your customers post to their social media sites about your products. This makes marketing your products much easier, since you can do it on two fronts.

If you ever get confused, there are plenty of ways to help you figure the theme out. You'll have some handy documentation on the theme that will help you out and you can always contact the theme help center, which Shopify runs.

Beauty is definitely a great theme for anyone who has a lot of beauty products to sell. It's a graceful design and the navigation bar is on the side. You'll definitely want to check this one out and see if it's right for you.

New Standard

This theme is a little different from the others. For one, the theme has a dark background, which isn't something that you see in a lot of the themes. Many of them stay on the lighter side. It has a sophisticated look, something that you can really tie to your products.

It's definitely a minimalistic theme, but that doesn't mean that there aren't tons of features for you to look at and mess with. Plus, if you aren't a big fan of the darker look, there are quite a few different color choices to choose from, including lighter options.

There are some features that people have said aren't available, including posting a welcome message or a video on the main page. These things aren't the end of the world, but if they are something you are looking forward to, maybe you should look at a different theme.

New Standard tries to create a new standard of themes. The dark background to this one is very different from the others, but it doesn't mean that it will be the right one for you. Check it out and see if you want to implement this one into your shop.

Kickstand

I wonder what this theme could possibly be about! This is obviously a great theme for a Kickstarter campaign. Any product you have that requires a Kickstarter will work perfectly in this handy theme.

This theme can help promote and sell anywhere up to five items. You'll have more than enough ability to really promote these items thanks to this theme. It's a very elegant theme that is visually pleasing.

What's even better is that with each item you have, you can have your full focus on that item. If you had two different items, for example, one wouldn't get more focus than the other. In fact, you'd be able to have the focus be on both of them. No one item will get more focus than the other, so both will have an equal chance of getting a customer to buy it.

You'll be able to talk about each of your products in great detail, even down to why you believe it was something that needed to be made. This sort of talking is something many people take to heart. It might be the reason they buy it, even if it isn't the most beneficial thing to them. If it is, then your passion behind the product will definitely influence them to tell everyone about it.

While you don't need to have a product be on Kickstarter to use this theme, it is useful for those who do. It's not every day that you have a theme that allows you to fully promote a Kickstarter product. When you find themes like this, especially free ones, you definitely need to check them out.

Annabelle

This theme isn't built by Shopify, but is built by a community member in the Shopify area. Annabelle is very versatile, working for many different products rather than a select few. On the main page of this theme, there is a large slider that can be incredibly useful. If you want, you can show off some of your favorite collections or maybe a sale that's happening within a collection.

Above this slider, there is a navigation bar that will lead to your various collections. Below the slider, however, there are three mini banners, which can say any number of things. These could be where your sales are shown or where another promotion you have is shown.

On every product page, there are a bunch of extra things that are extremely helpful. There's a place for your customers to write reviews on the product, which might influence someone to buy that product in the future. If you need it, there's room for a sizing chart. There's also a place where any related products will be shown.

Sometimes, customers really want to see a close up of the product you're trying to sell them. With this theme, they'll be able to hover over the photos of your products and get that closer view they desire.

You can have four, nine, twelve, or twenty products shown on each page at once. If you have less products, showing four a page might make it seem like there's more. If you have a lot, try going for twelve. At the same time, you don't want to clutter the page, so unless you have a lot of products, try to stay away from twenty if you can.

Also on the collection page, you can customize how big the icons are. If you want one of them featured, you could always make that one a lot larger. Or, maybe you want the dynamic as a whole to be fun and different. You could make the icons various sizes, making it fun to look at.

Annabelle is a strong free theme. It is full of features that you might need in your shop. The versatility of this theme makes it perfect for nearly anyone, so definitely check it out and see if it's the right one for you.

Fleur de Lis

Have you dreamed of having your own floral business? This theme might be exactly what you need to bring that dream to life. This is a unique theme that is specifically made for florists and their designs. It can be used in conjunction with an actual business, showing your creations to a wider audience.

The main page is full of different amazing features. Your customers won't have to navigate their way to the products you make, but only have to scroll down the page. There are a bunch of unique rows where you can show your products. All your customers will have to do is hit the arrow at the end of the row to see more products in that collection.

These rows don't all have to be collections. You can also use these rows to write about your products. You could even have an about section, which lets your potential customers know why you decided to do this or where your business originated. There are tons of ideas that you can do with these rows.

There are ways to feature certain products or deals that you might have. You can also have your newest products show up in a specific spot, so everyone will know what you've added. There's also a spot to have blog posts and a place for featured reviews to be posted about your business.

If you have any upcoming events, you can always use one of your rows to talk about those events. That way, anyone who lives near you or the event will be able to see your work at the event.

Though Fleur de Lis is mostly aimed towards those who are florists, you can probably make it work for other items as well. With a little work, this theme can become versatile, and might be exactly what you need. Definitely check it out and see if it works for you.

Focus

Here's another wonderful, minimalistic theme. As the name suggests, this theme really focuses your attention on your brand. Items that are similar will strive with this theme. If you sell tea and tea products, Focus would work great for you.

There are three unique color schemes that come with this theme: Eco, Focus, and Craftsman. Each of these presets comes with a slight variation in the color and the font used for the title. They all have a different feel as well, which is incredibly helpful when narrowing down your theme.

This theme allows for large scale images, which is very necessary with certain products. This theme is great for a wide range of things, including wood products, art supplies, or electronic accessories. It's always good when a theme is incredibly versatile and it makes the entire process much easier.

Do you have a newsletter attached to your business? It's very easy to implement a place for your customers to sign up for the newsletter with their email. They'll get all the latest sales and promotions in their emails, meaning they'll never be left out.

The navigation bar on top is perfect for getting your customers from point A to point B. Some ideas for what you can put on the bar is an about us page, your collection page, and maybe a place for your blog posts to show up. Since this is more about your brand, it's best if you have only a few products rather than a lot. The more you have, the less beneficial this theme will be.

Focus is a great theme for smaller businesses or those who want to focus on their brand. There's a lot you can do with this theme, but it does have its limitations. Be sure to check it out if you want a theme that is simple, but elegant.

Cheeser

This is a great theme for a store selling pet products. It was named after Grumpy Cat, so you know it's perfect for pet stores. You can sell plenty of different things in your store, including toys and other pet essentials.

It's a very simple setup and very easy to look at. For some, it might seem a little childlike, but it goes with the theme of pets. There is a side column on the left side where you can put any information that you want, including tags to help your customers find certain products easier.

Also on that side column is a place to write about your shop. You can say why you came up with it and what you plan on doing with it in the future, if you have major plans for it.

Cheeser is a cute little theme that is perfect for people who sell any pet related items. You can customize it enough to make it unique to your tastes. It might not have an amazing main page, but it's still worth checking out.

Gift Shop

This is definitely an interesting theme. It has a unique feel to it that other themes on this list don't have. The navigation bar on the side is the main source of navigation for your customers. Thankfully, it's a static sidebar, so even as they scroll down the page, they will be able to access it without any problems.

If you have a small to medium sized inventory, this theme works wonderfully. There's a search bar on the side bar so if your customers know what they want, they can find it quickly and easily.

The animation of the side bar is a nice touch as well. Any links on the side bar can be made into multi-level selections when hovering over them. You'll be able to easily separate your inventory in whatever sections are necessary.

Right on top, there is a place to have a slideshow. You can show off some of your various products here or show off any promotions you might have. The great thing about slideshows is that you can put whatever you need in it that will make your shop run smoothly.

It is extremely easy for many different kinds of products to be used in this theme. It can range from actual gift items to something like utensils. There is a nice amount of versatility in this theme, making it good for many people.

On the bottom, the footer has a place where you can put different links. You could add your business' social media or links to other things. You can also have a place for newsletter signup, so all of your customers can be kept up to date with your shop. Also, there's a great place to put your contact information as well.

Gift Shop is fairly versatile. While it might not have the same versatility as some of the others, the look of this theme is very nice. It has a more fun feeling than others and does have a slightly less sophisticated look. However, not every theme should feel like you pulled it out of a magazine. This could be the perfect theme for you, so definitely check it out.

Paid Themes for Shopify

No matter how much you might not want to pay for a theme, sometimes it's for the best. Some of these premium themes might speak to you in a way that the free themes just don't. Also, free themes can only do so much for you before an upgrade feels necessary. As your business grows, you should grow with it.

Sports Store

Can you even begin to figure out what this theme focuses on? It's exactly what the name suggests. This is a great theme for you to focus on your sports equipment. The great thing about this theme is it's not only for equipment, but clothing, shoes, and accessories as well.

Do you sell items for a specific sport? If that's the case, you can easily do that here. What if you sell more generically and sell workout equipment? That's also perfect for this theme. You aren't limited to any specific thing, but can focus a little more on what you want.

The demo of this theme focuses on workout equipment and clothing over any specific sport, but it would be easy to do that as well. Take tennis, for example. You could easily sell rackets and tennis balls, but you could extend that by adding different types of ball hoppers, an automatic ball shooting machine, and clothing. Also, getting specific shoes will definitely help as well.

You could also add braces or other sorts of equipment to help with pain or to prevent old injuries from flaring up. There are endless possibilities with what you can put into this theme.

The best thing about this theme is that it is made with navigation in mind. When you have an online store with a lot of products and equipment, you want navigation to be easy. You don't want to get lost, trying to find the thing you want. This theme comes with a side bar and a multi-level bar on top. Your customers won't be getting lost any time soon.

There's plenty of room on the header and footer for whatever information you need to put on it. You can have links on the footer to various things, like support and ways to like your social media pages. There are tons of possibilities for this theme.

Sports Store is a great theme if you have a huge inventory for anything. It can be electronics, sports, or anything that has a lot of different elements to it. For a single site, this can be purchased for $139. It's a great investment, so you should definitely check it out.

TheShop

Here's a great, responsive theme with multiple main pages to choose from. This is perfect for fashion and clothing stores. There are a ton of features with this theme that will make it more than worth it to buy.

There are three different main pages that you can choose from, each laid out slightly differently. They all have the same basic information on the first page, so picking one over the other doesn't mean you'll lose anything valuable.

The first main page, for example, has a search bar where the shopping cart icon is on the other two. The shopping cart is moved onto the bar at the top of the page instead. All three have a slideshow on top of the page, but the first main page has a promotional bar over the top of the slideshow. This promotional bar is below the slideshow in the second and split up into four small boxes instead.

When picking a main page with this theme, it all comes up to personal preference and what you think looks the best. You want the main page to have the functionality that you need along with looking really nice. Thankfully, no matter which one you choose, you'll have a great looking theme.

Do you want to have a blog with your shop? You can have a full page in your theme dedicated to your blog. Then, all of your customers would have a great place to go to if they had any questions about your store. Plus, you could easily give updates about anything you'll be adding to the shop or anything that you will be doing with the shop.

Of course, there is also a place for anyone to subscribe to your shop. From there, they could get email updates on anything happening with your shop, including any blog posts you might post. No matter what, with this theme, your customers will know what's happening with your shop.

Social media that is connected to your shop can easily be linked on the main page of your theme. It's a great way for your customers to know what they need to know when they need to know it.

When it comes to the actual product page, you can have a few photos of your products that, when hovered over, get a zoomed in view. You can also have a place to choose a different color of the item, a description of the item, a size chart, the return policy, and reviews of that specific item. Below that box is any related products in the store that might interest your customer. No matter where they are in the store, they'll always be able to find what they need.

The navigation system is very good as well. In the catalog page, there is a side bar that allows your customers to become very specific about what they're looking for. The can looked based on product type, color, price, size, and brand, if necessary. They won't have to worry about getting lost in your site.

TheShop might be one of the best premium clothing themes. There is so much you can do with it and so much you can add to it. There are tons of options and features that might not be in other themes. It's worth checking out if fashion is what you're selling. For only $49, this theme can be yours.

Ap Strollik

If you're selling a single product and want an incredibly reliable theme, this theme is perfect for you. Everything you need to promote your product is available in this theme.

On the main page, there's tons of stuff you can do. You can have your product description along with any highlights of this product. This will show your customers why this products is better than similar products out there. You can also go in depth about your product and bring your customers to a separate page, which goes through all of the aspects of your product.

Are there some key features about your product that makes it worth the price? You can list them out beside a photo of your product. These key features might be the reason a customer decides to buy your product rather than pass it by for another, similar product by someone else.

Do you have some customer reviews you want to show on the front page? There's a place for that. There's also a place where you can show different models of your product and show their prices. After reading through everything about your product, they might want to see the prices and make a decision.

An added bonus in this theme is the 360 view of your product. Instead of have tons of different photos of different angles, you can have one 360 view for your customers to look at.

They can see all the angles of your product without needless photos.

A blog is easy with this theme. All of your customers can read through it and get the story of the creation of your product. They can get a sense of how much you've been working to get this product out to the masses. You can also have a story page, where people tell their stories about using the product. Customers generally want to hear what other people's opinions are of the product before they make a final decision.

At the bottom of the main page, there's a great place for any customer to send your business any questions they might have that aren't answered. There is also a place to put your contact information and a place to put links throughout your store. They won't have to scroll all the way back up to go where they need to go.

You can also have a gallery of different images of your product. It can be your product in use or any way that your product will look as beneficial as it should be. If there are any accessories that might go with your product, you can also sell them using this theme. There are plenty of different categories to choose from using the navigation bar at the top of the screen.

The product page lists the price, any different colors it might have, and if it's available. Below that, there is a box that has a description, features of that product, and reviews. In the description box, you can actually add a video so your customers can see the product being used.

Related products are shown below the description box. If the product shown isn't quite what they want, they will easily be able to find something similar, but slightly different. They won't have to go searching through your entire site to find what they need.

Ap Strollik is a great theme for a single product promotion. Even though you are promoting that single product, it doesn't mean any accessories are forgotten. You can sell everything that goes with that product using this theme. If this is something that really works for you, you should definitely check it out. For only $56, it's well worth it.

Zidane

This theme has tons of features that can be implemented into many different types of products. You can use this for fashion, if you desired. Even something like e-cigarettes, which is what the demo shows, can be the product of choice in this theme.

There are three different homepages. Each has a slightly different look, just like with TheShop. Once again, these all have slight differences that might be exactly what you want for your shop. The slideshow at the top of the screen is slightly different for every homepage. For the first and third, it takes up a pretty large portion of the top of the page. For the middle, it's much smaller and brings the attention more to the menu on top and the featured products below.

All three of them have a search bar on top to look throughout the store for anything that you know the name of. On the second and third, there is a banner which says how many products the store has sold. This could be a fun thing to add when you get tons of sales. It also helps comfort people in knowing that others have purchased this product.

You can have a spot to talk about your product on the main page as well. It can be a short paragraph that explains some of the benefits of your product. On the first homepage option, you can also have a place to scroll through some reviews. This can be helpful for your customers to see as well.

When hovering over any of your products, you can choose to add it to your cart, save it to your wishlist, or get a quickview of the product. The quickview has a short description, the price, some pictures, and the ability to add it to your cart. It's pretty easy for customers to use this feature while shopping so they don't have to go back and forth between pages.

In the actual product page, the usual things, like price and photos, are there. There is also a more in depth description of the product and reviews of the product. Customers can also share the product to any of their social media pages using the buttons underneath.

Zidane has a lot of great features for whatever product you want to sell. The unique homepages can really make a difference in what people think of your products and what feeling they get from them. For only $56, it's a great choice for a theme page. Definitely check it out and see if it's right for you.

Jewelry

If you need a theme for selling jewelry, this one is great for you. You can also easily sell perfume or accessories with this one as well. There are tons of possibilities for your website using this theme.

There are for preset color schemes with this theme. The really cool thing about this is that these colors can be switched with the click of a button. You don't need to know any crazy coding or anything else. All you need to know is what color scheme you want. The navigation bar in this theme is massive. If you want to look at your catalog, hover over the word on the bar and the massive menu will show up.

This makes all of your categories easy to find. You won't have to worry about people getting confused or lost, since everything will be easily found on that menu. A cool addition to this is that you can have multiple currencies. This way, your shop can reach a lot of people.

On your products, you can put little badges on your product photos. This will allow you to say what products are new or have a sale. These are small badges, but they are just eye-catching enough for someone to see them.

Your customers can continuously add products to their shopping cart throughout their shopping experience. Also, on your main page, you can have a gallery of some of your products. Your customers will be able to check out your products as soon as they get on your page. From there, they'll have an idea of what you're selling right off the bat and know if they want to continue looking at your site.

Your customers will be able to look at your products in whatever way they want, including a grid view or a list view. This really helps people who want to have as much customization as possible. You can also look at them alphabetically, by best-selling, or by price. All of these help make it so much better and you don't even have to reload the page to change them.

Blog posts are a great way to keep your customers up to date on everything with your business. If you have any promotions or anything like that, all of your customers will be able to find things they need through your blog post. Your contact information and your location, if you have a physical store. Plus, Google fonts are included in this, so you'll be able to change the fonts to what you want.

Jewelry is a wonderful theme that you can do a lot with. There are plenty of features to choose from and you can really customize this to exactly what you need. For only $139, this can be your new theme. You should definitely check this out if you think this one might help you.

Extreme

Do you sell sports equipment? Maybe it's for snowy weather sports or maybe it's for some sort of extreme sport. This one will be a great theme for all of these things. There are a lot of amazing features in this that might just be exactly what you need.

Responsive themes are a must and this is definitely a responsive theme. Just like with the last one, this has a mega menu, making your customers have an easy time finding the product they want. There are also four great color schemes that you can choose from. All of these are great and vibrant, making them perfect to choose from.

Do you have a promotion going on? Then you can add a promo banner to let everyone know how long your sale will be going on and exactly what it will be for. All of this can really make the difference in if someone stays on your site or not.

Newsletters can be a wonderful addition to your business. You can set a pop-up for a newsletter so everyone who goes to your store will see it. There is also a slider on top of the page where you can put any important information that you want everyone to see.

Your customers can add things to their carts while they shop. They will be able to find something they want and just click on the cart icon. It will automatically be added to the cart. You will also be able to scale your font to whatever you want without losing any quality in your fonts.

Blogs and a contact form are also part of this theme. It will help you keep in contact with all of your customers and make sure they know how to contact you. As long as they have this information available, they will always be able to contact you.

Extreme is a wonderful theme that has a lot of potential. There are tons of different things you can do with it, including making sure your promotions are widely seen. At a price of $139, it's a great theme that you'll be able to really make work for your shop.

Tea Store

Maybe tea is your thing. This would be a great theme for not only tea, but a wide variety of different things. Candles might be a good thing to sell as well or even bath products. There are tons of things that would really work with this.

You can have a mega menu in this one, but it's on the side instead of on the top. This is a great addition that helps make the homepage look even better than before. There are a lot of great things about this theme, including something called a parallax. This is a 2D image that is made to give it a bit of a depth. It basically is two layers. The first is your background, the one that you see. The second is a complimentary solid color that helps bring out the rest of your background.

There are color changes that you can do with one click. They are bright colors that are complimentary with something like tea or bath products. There's a lot you can do with those colors and make them work for your products.

A great addition is a background video. This is part of your background, which makes it active and a lot of fun to look at. It's definitely different and might just make a customer stay and look at other products you have. This video might also be a way to tell a story, which is also a very fun thing to do. It can really help boost your sales.

All of your products have the ability to have mini badges on them, which can promote a sale or say that a product is new. All of these are great for making sure your customers know exactly what's up.

If you have any products that you want to showcase, you are more than able to do. Right on the home page, you'll be able to showcase whatever products you want in a sophisticated way that looks really good. It also looks incredibly organized, which is always a great thing to have, especially on your home page.

There is a quick view option with this theme as well. Customers will be able to click on any product and get a quick view of it if they want to. This will allow them to quickly look at the product, but not have to leave the page to look at it. One last great thing about this theme is it doesn't matter what browser your customer uses, they'll be able to use it without issue.

Tea Store is a wonderful theme that can do a lot of different things. You won't have to worry about your customers getting confused or lost with the great navigation system. For only $139, this theme can be the new background for your business site. Make sure to check it out if you think it might be the one for you.

Computers

It's a complete mystery as to what this could possibly be for. Computers is a great theme to use if you sell anything to do with computers. There are some great colors you can choose from, including a beautiful green and a luscious blue. They are some great colors that can really make your site pop.

On the top of the home page, there's a great slider that can help showcase some of your products that you might want your customers to see. This is a wonderful way for your customers to see what some of your biggest products are or the ones you think represent your company.

If you want, you can set the prices per currency. This can be beneficial in making sure they are all set appropriately to the price of the product. Also, this theme has documentation which can tell you everything you might need to know about the theme, including how to set up your theme to make it work the way you want it to.

Any time you have any sales or new products, you can give any product that needs it a little badge. That will allow everyone to know exactly what products are on sale with a quick glance. It saves a lot of time for people if they can just look and know.

On the home page, there's a place to showcase a ton of different products you have. It's an organized way that looks great and doesn't take away from your overall page. In fact, it only adds to it and it could be the reason people stick around.

The mega menu is great and is also considered a sticky menu. Every time you hover over the menu, a huge menu will come out which has extra places to go to. This makes it even better for businesses with a lot of inventory. No matter what, they'll be able to find their way.

Computers might be the theme that you've been looking for. If you sell any sort of electronic equipment, this will really help you sell that equipment. The price on this is only $139 and is definitely one you should check out.

Mozar

Here's another great fashion theme which is perfect for any sort of fashion or clothing. It's a very clean looking theme that is great for modern clothes. Along with that, there are also other things you can do, including jewelry, flowers, cooking equipment, furniture, sports, and other stuff.

There are two different layouts for the home page, both of which you can choose from. There is a slideshow right on the first page that shows whatever you want to showcase. It could be products that really speak to your brand or ones that are on sale. The possibilities are endless.

Both of these home pages have plenty of things that you can mess with. The second home page has banners throughout the home page where you can add some things about your business. If you want, it can be any promotions that you might have or something else that's beneficial to them.

The mobile version is very smooth and is definitely attainable for anyone. You can do a lot with this and make it a great theme for your business website. This is a great responsive theme that works extremely well.

This theme is fully compatible with every major browser you might use, so you don't have to worry about it not working on a different browser. You also have Google font, so you can change your font to whatever is allowed in Google fonts.

Mozar might be the theme that you need to make your website pop. It is a great and multi-featured theme and for only $56, it's definitely a great theme you should check out.

Arion

Furniture might be your forte. If that's the case, then Arion is a great theme for you. It looks very modern and sleek, which can give your business a great boost. There is a ton of stuff you can do with this one as well.

Your customers will be easily able to look at your products with the quick view. This way, they'll be able to click on the product and get a quick look at the product. This will tell them the price and a short description. The best thing about this is that they don't even have to leave the page they're looking at.

This theme is incredibly easy to install and to customize to your needs. You don't have to be a coding genius to make this work. In fact, all you need to do is read the documentation that comes with it and you'll be set. If you're still having trouble after, you can always contact the creator to get some extra help.

There is a full wishlist support with this theme. All of your customers will be able to have everything on their wishlist that they want. If there is anything loyal customers like, it's being able to save everything that they want to get in the future.

This has a wonderful setup. The home page has everything you could want on it, including a place for testimonials and your blog posts. There's also plenty of places where you can split up your products based on different categories. On the home page, there is also a spot to have a banner where you can write if there's a sale or not, along with other things.

The top has a nice navigation bar that has plenty of space for a lot of places you have to go to. There is a lot you can do with this mega menu and it will make navigation a breeze for your customers.

The product pages themselves have a box for a description and reviews others have made about this product. There is also a list of related products underneath that. Any colors that you can choose for the product, along with the price, a few photos, and what category they're in, are also on this page.

Arion might just be the theme a furniture guru needs. There's a lot that can be done with this theme and plenty of ways to use it as well. You won't have angry customers when looking at this theme, that's for sure. This theme is only $56 and is well worth checking out. It might just surprise you.

Quartz

If there is a theme that is meant for many different ideas, this is it. Flowers, toys, jewelry, beauty, and equipment are all possibilities with this theme. You might not find a theme that is quite as versatile as this one.

This one has a large search bar at the top of the page. Your customers will easily be able to look for anything they need that is in your store. If they know what they need but don't want to search through the entire store, then they can use this search bar.

The home page features plenty of places for you to have various categories of your products, including a featured section. Also, there is a slideshow right on top of the page, which is incredibly beneficial for showing off some of your featured products or any promotions you might be having.

Breaking up the different categories of information are some banners, which can have sales or have a new line of products you've just introduced. There are tons of possibilities for these banners and they are a nice way to give you customers some extra information they might not otherwise see.

Also on your homepage, on the right side, is a place where you can show some blog posts, top sellers, FAQ's, and even more banners with information. The home page of this theme is full of various information, some of which will be extremely beneficial to your customers on their search of your store.

A quick view of any product in your store will make your customers lives much easier. They won't have to leave the page to get some information on the product, but only have to click on the quick view. It will give them the necessary information that will help them decide if they want to learn more about the product. It's a great way to inform your customer without making them jump through hoops.

In the corner of any product, you can have a mini banner which can indicate a product that is new, on sale, or a top seller. Really, these mini banners can make the products stick out in any way possible, so it's a great idea to utilize those.

Quartz is a wonderful theme that might be exactly what you need for whatever products you sell. You could even sell an assortment of products using this theme. There are endless possibilities and for only $56, this can be the theme for you. Check it out and make sure it's perfect.

Mosaic

This is an amazing theme for any kind of artistry or fashion. The theme is dominated by photos, which are all high quality photos. If you are selling your own art, this theme will be perfect.

It has a place where you can talk about a piece you are currently working on. This might get a customer hyped enough to make an offer before it is completed. Even if no one does, it can still generate some traffic to your site. They want to see the progress you make on the art and as long as you keep it updated regularly, they'll keep coming back.

If you would rather do a video for your current work, that's also possible. You could make a speed video of something you're making so everyone can see how you work. This will give them a great idea of how you go about your day, making incredible art.

Your latest pieces or ones that you are particularly proud of can go right at the top of the page. They'll be the first thing your customer sees, so if they like that, they might just keep looking. A great thing about this theme is that you can sell original work or sell prints of your work. You aren't stuck with anything in particular.

On the product page, there is a related products part at the bottom of the page. Any piece of art that is similar in some way to the one they are viewing will show up at the bottom. It will help bring your customers to all of your work that they might be interested in.

Your customers will easily be able to share your products on social media. There isn't much they have to do except click a button and log into their account. This can really help promote your business and bring it to the masses.

Mosaic is a great, photography based, theme. There is a lot you can do with it and you definitely won't regret checking it out. Plus, it's only $180 and it's a great thing to spend that much on.

Lorenza

For a fashion store, this one is a great choice. Boutique retailers will especially love the look of this theme. In fact, it might be the perfect choice for your store. There is a lot that can be done with this theme and all of it is good.

This has an asymmetrical layout. It won't look as boxy and normal looking as a lot of other websites, but will have a unique design that fits things like boutiques very well. This layout is a great way to be aesthetically pleasing without being overboard.

Do you like having a bar across the top of your page with all of the menu items? Or, would you rather have the simple three lined icon that hides the menu? This theme allows you to choose which one you would rather have. It's a great idea to try out both and figure out which one you feel works better for your store.

There is an icon used to sign up for your store's newsletter, if you have one. Newsletters are a great way to get your customers up to speed on everything going on in your store. It's also a great way to keep loyal customers coming back. Right by the newsletter icon is a search icon. This will let your customers search the whole store with the click of a button and a few keystrokes.

Large product images are easy with this theme. They look great and work really well with the theme. They are the reason why fashion is a great fit with this theme. The focus is on the photos for sure.

There are three great styles you can choose from for this theme: handmade, heritage, and urban. All of these have a great color scheme. It's up to you which one fits your shop the best. Try them all out and see which one you end up liking the best.

Social media feeds from Instagram and Twitter are super easy to do with this theme. You won't have to worry at all about your customers missing out on your shops latest deals or anything else thanks to these feeds.

Lorenza is a strong contender in the best theme for fashion and clothing. In fact, if you have $160 to spend, this might be exactly what one you should choose. It works incredibly well and you should definitely check it out.

Palo Alto

A modern theme might be what you're looking for. If it is, Palo Alto is the perfect one for you. There's a lot to it that you'll love.

For one, the overlapping photos are a beautiful addition that helps this theme stand out from the plethora of other themes out there.

There are three unique styles that you can choose from with this theme, which include Palo Alto, SoMa, and Stanford. These are all, of course, places in California, so it gives your products a pretty interesting feeling.

There is a very contemporary style attached with this theme and it's perfect for small inventories. You can easily put products that are similar in this theme, like skateboards or wooden toys. This theme is perfect for building up your brand, especially if you're a small business.

On your homepage, you can feature reviews people have said about your business, which can help influence others to buy your products if they know you're reliable. Right below the customer reviews, you can have a thing set up for newsletters. All your customers have to do is type their email in and they will be entered onto the email list. They'll never miss a sale or a new product as long as they are on that.

You can add a video onto your home page, which gives your potential customers an idea of what kind of products you sell and why these products are important. Plus, throughout the page, you can give little tidbits about your products and maybe why you wanted to sell them in the first place.

The product page is rather simple, showing the price, quantity, a short description, and some photos. There are other themes that have more to their product pages, but for a smaller inventory, these things might not be entirely necessary.

Of course, there is also a page for you to have blog posts. In case someone doesn't want a newsletter, they can always check your blog for anything they might want to know. You can post about a big sale you plan on having with a few of your products or a store wide sale. Plus, any new items can be blogged about as well.

Palo Alto has a lot of great features that businesses with small inventories will love to use. They will make your start-up business much easier than they might normally have been. This theme is only $180, so you should check it out if this sounds like your type of theme.

Themes are no doubt an incredibly important part of your Shopify website. There are a lot themes need to be able to do in order for your shop to be truly successful, including having the features you need and having enough space for a bigger or smaller inventory.

Also, having easy to use navigation makes a world of a difference with your site. If your theme's navigation doesn't make sense or just doesn't work, people will go to another site to find what they need. If you can make the customer's life easy, then they might just become your next most loyal customer.

There are tons of themes that have been listed and once you know if you want to pay money or not, you should check all of them out. One of them is bound to be the perfect fit for your brand and the products you sell.

CHAPTER FIVE

UNDERSTANDING DROP SHIPPING AND ITS RELATION WITH SHOPIFY

For selling a product online and especially through Shopify, drop shipping plays a great role in it. Let's first understand what drop shipping refers to. It is basically a method related to retail fulfillment in which a retailer is not the actual owner of the inventory sold by him.

After receiving the order from the customer, the requirement is passed to the merchant by the retailer who delivers the product after fulfilling the order. In the whole process, the retailer never deals with the product himself.

So, what's the difference between drop shipping and the standard retail model? The primary difference is that one doesn't need to manage or buy the inventory up front which helps in saving a huge amount for the company.

Let's know about the merits of drop shipping which helps in enhancing one's business growth perspectives to a large extent. In fact, it has a lot of benefits which can certainly help in building as well as growing one's business.

Merits of Drop shipping

Requirement of Less Capital– It is one of the biggest merits of drop shipping. In this, your huge amount of capital is not blocked for managing and buying inventory. In fact, that's also the main reason behind a number of start-ups finding a wonderful option in drop shipping for selling their products.

Sail Smoothly – Yes, it's selling as well as sailing smoothly with drop shipping as there are various factors which you just don't need to bother about with drop shipping. Some of those factors include:

- Managing or making payment for a warehouse

- Shipment and packing of your orders

- Tracking of inventory for accounting risks

- Inbound shipments and handling issues related to returns

- Ordering products consistently and organizing stock level

Minimum Overhead Expenses – As there is no involvement of the inventory cost, the overhead expenses are very low in this. In the initial phase, many successful drop shipping businesses have been run from home using just a laptop and an expense of only $100 per month.

No Location Issue- As a drop shipping business can be easily operated from any part of the world, there is no issue related to choosing a good location for doing business in this. All you need to have is good internet speed for flourishing your business at a good pace.

Wide Range Product Selections – As you are not bound to keep a stock of your products in this, you can actually provide a plethora of options to your customers. This means you won't be stuck with only a few things you can sell. Your inventory will be larger and will likely draw more people to your store.

High Scalability- Scalability becomes a big concern in most of the traditional businesses. However, while using the drop shipping method, you need not bother about this. In fact, it helps in developing your business with less pain as well as less incremental work.

Undoubtedly, the changing times have made drop shipping a lucrative option for the businesses.

Is Drop shipping Worth It?

The fact can't be denied that drop shipping is a great model for start-ups. Yes, everything comes with its own pros and cons , but the merits of drop shipping overpower any of its demerits if it has.

So, go ahead and build a profitable drop shipping business. With careful planning, you can definitely turn out to be a successful ecommerce businessman with drop shipping.

Drop shipping Is a Service, Not a Position

It is to be understood that "drop shipper" isn't one of the positions mentioned in the supply chain. There must be a question in your mind, Why? It is due to the reason that retailer, wholesaler or manufacturer; anyone can play the role of a drop shipper.

The Order Process:

Let's understand how a drop shipping business work with an example-

Phone Outlet or a theoretical store is an online merchant who holds expertise in accessories required for smartphones. A phone outlet does a good job in wholesale accessories as all its products are drop shipped directly from a wholesaler. This is also the reason behind the usage of the term wholesale accessories.

Let's understand the process of the whole order process step by step:

Step 1 –An Order is Placed by the Customer with Phone Outlet
Mr. John requires a cover for his new Smartphone, and he places an order through the online store of the phone outlet. After the approval of the order, the process followed is as follows -

- Both Phone Outlet and Mr. John get an automatically generated email confirmation regarding the new order by the store software.

- The payment of Mr. John payment captured during the checkout process will be automatically deposited into the bank account of the phone outlet.

Step 2 – Order placed with supplier by the Phone Accessory Outlet
After this, the email order confirmation is forwarded to a sales representative at wholesale accessories by the phone accessory outlet. Wholesale Accessories which already has phone outlet's credit card on file will bill it for the wholesale price of the goods. It will include any shipping or processing fees as well.

Note: Some drop shippers may support automatic XML which is a common format used for inventory files while uploading orders. However; email is the most convenient as well as the common way to place orders with drop shipping suppliers.

Step 3 – Order is Shipped by Wholesale Accessories

After the completion of the above steps, the wholesaler gives confirmation about the required inventory in stock. Then, he boxed up the order, and it is directly shipped to the customer. Address and name of the phone outlet will be mentioned on the address label for return even when the shipment comes from Wholesale Accessories. The logo of the phone outlet will also be mentioned on the packing slip as well as the invoice.

After the finalization of the shipment, an email with the invoice and a tracking number will be sent by the wholesale accessories to the phone outlet.

Note: The turnaround time for drop shipped orders is quite fast. Many times an order is delivered within a few hours. Due to this, merchants also advertise same-day shipping though they use a drop shipping supplier.

Step 4 – Customers Informed about the Shipment by Phone Outlets

After receiving the tracking number, Phone Outlet sends the tracking information to the customer.

The order is considered to be complete after the shipment of the order, collection of the payment and notification to the customer regarding the same.

So, if we have to find out the final profit or loss in this order, it can be calculated by the difference amount charged to Mr. John and the payment made to wholesale accessories.

Where is the Dropshipper in the Picture? Completely Invisible

Instead of playing a significant role in the whole process, the customer remains completely unaware of the drop shipper. On the package received by the customer, only the return address and logo of the phone outlet will be mentioned. Incase Mr. John receives the wrong order, his first point of contact will be the phone outlet. Then, the phone outlet will further coordinate with the Wholesale Accessories in order to get the right item shipped to the customer.

In fact, the drop shipping wholesaler doesn't even exist for the end customer. His primary responsibility includes only stocking and shipping of products. Apart from that, everything else involved in the process like website development, customer service, and marketing remain the responsibilities of the merchant.

How to Pick the Right Niche

The biggest challenge faced by most of the new drop shipping entrepreneurs is to pick up the right product line to be focused. The blunder committed at this phase is to give importance to one's personal interests in choosing a niche as it doesn't help in any manner in the long run. Such strategies can only be acceptable when it ensures success in your business.

Becoming a Successful Online Seller

For building a successful ecommerce business, here are a few steps which can be followed by you:

Become a Manufacturer–When you manufacture your products, you get a chance to cut through the competition and quote a price according to your own wish. However, if you wish to drop ship products, existing products will be sold by you which will be actually manufactured by someone else.

Distribution Benefit or Exclusive Pricing – With access to exclusive pricing benefit from a manufacturer, you get the opportunity to sell online while earning good profits without creating your own product. These arrangements may sound a bit tough in the initial phase as similar goods, and wholesale prices will be accessible to many other dropship merchants as well.

Sell at the Lowest Price - By offering the lowest price, you'll certainly get a big portion of business in the market.

However; if you don't have anything else to grab other's attention than low prices, then you may become a part of pricing war which may lead to lose your profits.

Add Value to Your Non-Pricing Terms – By getting expert advice and guidance within your niche can prove to be one of the best ways for building a profitable drop shipping business.

Add Value to Ecommerce –It's easier to say this, but certainly tough to achieve it. Various products and niches follow this strategy more than others. By choosing some key characteristics which may add value with educational content will make the selling of your products much easier.

Showcase more Components- When a product requires more components for its proper functioning, the chances of customers looking for the functioning of various components of the internet will increase. So, more components add more variety to the product giving greater opportunity to add value by advising customers about the compatibility of the different components of the products.

Highlight Relevant Information– On the availability of numerous options, customers generally get confused. Therefore, it is always recommended to add value to your business with the help of content. With this, you would be able to provide specific guidance on the type of products best suited for the specific environment. In fact, it will also provide proper guidance while keeping in view the needs of the customers.

Technical Setup Support on Installation – It is a great idea to provide expert guidance for products that customers generally find difficult to set up and install. For example- you are interested in buying a security camera. It's something which many find difficult to install. However; if you find a detailed 50-page installation guide on a site also telling about the mistakes made by people while installing cameras, you would prefer buying it from that website even if other sites provide the product at a lower price. In fact, most of us would prefer that in order to save time as well as difficulty in installation.

How to Add Value

Here are a few tested ways to add value to your complicated niches:

- By creating comprehensive guides for buyers

- By providing detailed product descriptions

- By offering installation and setup guides

- By creating videos showing the working of the product as well as the function of various components

- By establishing an easy system for understanding the compatibility of the components

How to Find the Right Customers

It's a fact that customers behave, think and buy in completely different ways keeping in view their varied budget and requirements. Mostly, it's seen that customers interested in buying small items demand the most expensive ones, while the potential big spenders remain away from buying even low-cost items.

For targeting the right customers for getting profit in your business, the demographic structure should always be kept in view.

Hobbyists Customers – People really passionate about their hobbies love to spend even hefty amounts for refining their skills. You must have heard how mountain bikers opt for bikes even more expensive than some luxurious cars. So, if you can find out the right hobbyists, you can successfully get some enthusiastic customers for your business.

Business Customers – You may find such customers more sensitive towards pricing as they prefer to place orders in bulk quantities, unlike other customers. After establishing a rapport with such customers, you can look forward to a highly profitable as well as a long-term relationship. In fact, you must try your best to sell products to businesses as well as individual customers.

Get Hold of Repeat Buyers – Who wouldn't like to have recurring revenue, a cycle which just goes on? Such possibilities increase if you choose such products for selling which are disposable or reordered frequently. It gives you a wonderful chance to build more loyal customers who would come back to you for making a purchase.

What All to Consider while Selecting a Product

The Ideal Price – The pricing structure should always be ideal to gain the confidence of the customers and make them feel comfortable while placing an order with your store. You also need to consider the fact that a customer will be more comfortable in placing an order of $200 even without chatting or talking to any representative on the phone. However, if a person is buying an item of $1,500, the person would definitely like to discuss with a sales representative or chat directly before finalizing the order placement with your store.

So, if you are selling high-priced items, you must have the option to provide personalized call support to your customers. However; it must also be ensured that the margins remain high enough even after providing the pre-sale support. Items ranging from \$50 to \$200 are considered to be the best for earning maximum revenue without the bindings of offering any extensive pre-sale support.

MAP Pricing – MAP pricing refers to minimum advertised price set up by some manufacturers for their products. It helps in preventing the price wars for products that are drop shipped easily to a large extent. It also ensures a reasonable profit for the merchants as they carry products directly from the manufacturer's end.

In case you find a niche where manufacturers have set upMAP pricing, it proves to be highly beneficial for such merchants who look forward to build an information-rich and high-value site. As prices will remain same for your competitors as well, you can give a tough competition to them on the strength of your website. In fact, you also won't have to lose profits because of less reputable business competitors.

Do Marketing In Advance – All plans regarding the marketing of your business and the channels to be used must be decided in advance. So, make a detailed plan for the promotion of your business before launching it. For example, tasks such as writing content, giving samples of products and engaging online communities who use your products for testimonials should be done in advance. With detailed research beforehand, you will be saved from the disadvantages of awful marketing.

For improving your overall margin, selling a product with a number of accessories is considered to be a profitable way.

More Accessories – As a general rule in retailing business, margins on lower priced accessories are higher as compared to the margins one can earn on high-priced items. A cell phone store may earn only a 5-10% margin on a Smartphone, but can easily make 100% or 200% margin on its cover.

The fact can't be denied that customers spend more time in making the decision for high priced items as compared to the low-priced ones. You would certainly do more online searches before buying an expensive smartphone than a case of a smartphone. In fact, you may buy the case from a local store near your place without much thought.

Investment on Website- Undoubtedly, an informative and high-quality site will pay bigger dividends. However, if the products sold by you change every year, maintaining that site would become difficult, and you will accumulate a huge amount of work for yourself. So, it's better to choose such products which don't get updated due to the launch of new models every year. This way, your invested time and money for the website won't go in vain.

Non-availability of Product Locally – It's a great way to earn a profit and increase your chances of success if you choose such products which are not available in the nearby locality. A garden rake or a sprinkler may be easily available anywhere, however; falcon training equipment or a medieval knight's costume will be hard to find. In fact, most people will go online to search its availability.

Smaller products mean lesser or no shipping costs – Everyone expects free shipping with online purchase. It becomes easier to give with smaller products as compared to the larger ones which charge hefty amounts for shipping. So, go for smaller items to give free shipping to your customers. Since they weigh a lot less, you'll be able to make sure shipping is way lower than it might normally be.

Measuring Demand

There can't be supply if there is no demand. In case you choose such a product which is not liked by anybody, you may end up losing all your investments and not earning any profits. As it's said and must be understood while doing any business that filling an existing demand is much easier than creating demand for a completely new product.

However; we all are fortunate enough that a number of online tools help in measuring the demand for any specific product easily and thus make it easier in choosing the product. The most renowned and reliable tool for this is the Google Keyword Tool.

Google Keyword Tool- It is considered one of the most efficient tools for entrepreneurs trying to set up their business nowadays. With the help of its keyword tool, Google helps you in calculating the number of people looking for your product online. You just need to type in a word or phrase related to your product and Google will show the result.

For the convenience of the users, Google also offers training modules so that anyone can use the tool effectively without any confusion.

Here are the three tips which must be kept in mind to make the best usage of the Google keyword tool:

- **Match Type** – With the help of the tool, you can choose broad, phrase or exact match types for knowing the search volumes. Through this, you will come to know the exact picture of the applicable search volume for the given keyword.

- **Search Location** – You must ensure that you check the local search volume and not the global search volumes.

It's because if you plan to sell your products in a specific region, the global search results will be of no use for you. So, you need to focus on local search volumes where your customers will be.

- **Long-Tail Variations** – People find it easier to use one or two-word search words for getting good search volume, however; the truth is that the longer and more specific terms get the highest traffic from the search engines. Such detailed search terms are popularly known as long-tail searches.

So, if you look forward to potential markets and niches for doing a successful business, you must choose a search term with maximum variations as that's what people actively search on search engines.

CHAPTER SIX

MAKING MONEY ONLINE WITH SHOPIFY

Now come the most lucrative part and in fact, we can say the thing for which everyone works. Yes, that is money. Shopify is a wonderful platform to make money online. Here is a brief description of a few ways to earn cash with Shopify.

Establish your own store

It is certainly one of the most significant ways to make money with Shopify. The primary requirement is just to have something to sell! If you are not the owner of traditional bricks and mortar business, you can certainly take help of Drop Shipping. Here are some of the guidelines for drop shipping:

Affiliate Program

In case you don't have your own products for selling and you are not even interested in drop shipping , you can join the Shopify affiliate program with which you to earn up to $358 per customer using the option of customer referrals. In this, you have two options to choose from:

1. **Earn Residual Income in the form of Revenue Share as Your Monthly Income**

   It's easy to earn commissions for all the Shopify customers referred by you on your website. The amount of commissions can go up to $35 per month.

2. **Earn Commission per Sale of a Client's subscription**

   The website traffic influences your income to a large extent as the promotional contents available on the sites motivate the customers doing online searches to buy the products and thus boost your sales.

Promote Shopify on Your Review Site

If you are not comfortable working on affiliate programs, you can make regular income just by running a review website on Shopify. It helps the customers in easily finding out the best and the most reliable products. In case your review website scores a high position in search engine rankings, it will certainly bring more Shopify sign ups to your site thereby helping to make more money. In order to gain such good income, you must have good traffic presence on your website which will help in enhancing the conversion rates.

Show Creativity in Shopify Themes

If you are a person with a creative bent of mind, you can make customized themes to grab the attention of the customers.

Create a Shopify App

It requires good programming skills. If you are good at it, you can design an App with the help of Shopify API and enhance the customer experience. Apps are a great way for your business to be mobile. You can not only have people looking at your products wherever they are, but they will also be able to quickly look and see if you've posted any updates.

The advantages of having an app are remarkable. You can not only make sure your customers are always up to date, but you can also make sure they know about any and all promotions and sales you'll be having. The advantages are great, as long as you have some way to make it.

Advantages of Using Shopify To Make Money

- Availability of Shopify packages at competitive rates.

- Availability a 14-day free trial demonstration.

- Free Ecommerce set up option.

- Easy to implement with GET STARTED option which provides an informative forum to get your site started in minutes. You just need to name your shop, add a short and catchy description to it specifying business contact details and the shop address.

- Even if you don't have products to sell, you can still make good amount using the Shopify affiliate program

How to Get more Sales on Social Media

Social media has been playing a pivotal role in boosting online sales nowadays. People make good use of the social media platform for making people aware about their products and grabbing their attention towards it.

For example, if you are interested in selling an iPhone case, the best way is to buy it from Everbuying for 4$ and then sell it for $10 keeping a margin of $6 at your Shopify store.

Not only this, but you can also create a discount code for 20% off and advertise it on Facebook, Twitter or Reddit for gaining the attention of more people towards it.

People love to buy gadgets using discount coupon codes and every day such sales are being done in huge numbers. Not only this, but you can also create Facebook stores and sell more products over there.

CONCLUSION

So, people who are looking forward to set up a successful online business empire, the Shopify platform is the best option. With a wide selection of premium templates offered by the site at affordable prices, you can easily build an attention-grabbing site for your online store. Not only this, with access to templates of CSS and HTML codes, you will also be able to customize the existing templates and create a completely new website for your ecommerce business with Shopify.

These templates, or themes, are incredibly beneficial to your shop. In fact, a lot of the time, these might be what brings even more customers in. Picking the right theme can be incredibly difficult, but if you choose wisely, whether it's paid or free, you'll be on your way to having a wonderful shop. Of course, picking a theme is only half of the work. You definitely need to make sure your customizations of the theme work really well for your shop.

The other two features that make Shopify stand apart and much above others are the availability of POS system and its fully integrated payment processor. It helps in handling your online transactions as well as processing in-person payments. Even if you are not keen to have a complete online store, Shopify Lite plan will help you in promoting your business and process credit card transactions via online mode as well as in person. With Shopify, you get both software and hardware necessary for running a retail business online as well as at a physical location.

Shopify doesn't limit your business to its own site but lets you flourish by selling products on other websites as well with the usage of Shopify Buy Buttons, or with the help of social networking sites such as Pinterest, Facebook, and Twitter.

The site also offers a convenient way to do business by organizing more than 1000 options available by grouping the apps into changing those into collections. It really makes the whole process easier and more efficient.

Apart from apps to enhance the functionality of your website, there are various other applications available for promoting your website, managing transactions, handling accounting, and everything else you can think of and required for running an online business successfully.

Free Bonus: Join Our Book Club and Receive Free Gifts Instantly

Click Below For Your Bonus:
https://success321.leadpages.co/freebodymindsoul/

Checkout My Other Books

http://amzn.to/2gf2ACP

40198902R00074

Made in the USA
Middletown, DE
05 February 2017